T0414382

WILD
EARTH
SCIENCE

TSUNAMIS

by Isaac Kerry

PEBBLE
a capstone imprint

Published by Pebble, an imprint of Capstone
1710 Roe Crest Drive, North Mankato, Minnesota 56003
capstonepub.com

Library of Congress Cataloging-in-Publication Data is available on the Library of Congress website.

ISBN: 9781663976987 (hardcover)
ISBN: 9781666327236 (paperback)
ISBN: 9781666327243 (ebook PDF)

Summary: Deep under water, something shifts. Ocean water pulls back from the shore. Then it comes flooding back. It's a tsunami! Learn about tsunamis, warning signs, and how to stay safe.

Editorial Credits
Editor: Ericka Smith; Designer: Tracy Davies; Media Researcher: Svetlana Zhurkin; Production Specialist: Katy LaVigne

Image Credits
Getty Images: Lloyd Cluff, 19, Rifo Reynaldo, 21; Newscom: Reuters/Kyodo, 4; Shutterstock: alybaba, 15, Ana del Castillo, 28, arda savasciogullari, 17, dynamic (map background), back cover and throughout, Falcon video, 5, Fotos593, 29, Frans Delian, 18, Kurniawan Rizqi, 9, lumyai I sweet, 7, Makoto_Honda, 26, Mana Photo, cover, 1, 3, Mimadeo, 11, Muhammad Qadri Anwar, 22, pashabo, cover (logo), Patara, 24, Sakarin Sawasdinaka, 27, Sky Cinema, 13, Tejasfilm.tv, 25, tunasalmon, 16, udaix, 8; U.S. Fish and Wildlife Service: Pete Leary, 23; USGS: Dr. Bruce Jaffe,14

TABLE OF CONTENTS

A Hundred-Foot-High Wave. . . . 4

What Is a Tsunami?. 6

Where in the World?. 16

Tsunami Dangers. 20

Being Prepared. 24

Tsunami Incoming!. 28

Glossary 30

Read More 31

Internet Sites 31

Index 32

About the Author 32

Words in **bold** are in the glossary.

A HUNDRED-FOOT-HIGH WAVE

A loud sound booms across the beach. A huge wave rushes in. It's a tsunami!

A tsunami hitting a city in Japan

Damage from a tsunami in Japan

Tsunamis are giant waves. They are one of nature's most dangerous events. They crash onto land. And they destroy what's in their path.

WHAT IS A TSUNAMI?

The word tsunami is Japanese. It means **"harbor** wave." Tsunamis happen when something moves a lot of water in the ocean. This creates waves. Those waves travel to the shore.

Imagine a plastic cup filled with water. If you tapped the bottom, a small wave would form on the top. It would start in the middle of the cup. Then it would move to the sides. Tsunamis work like this.

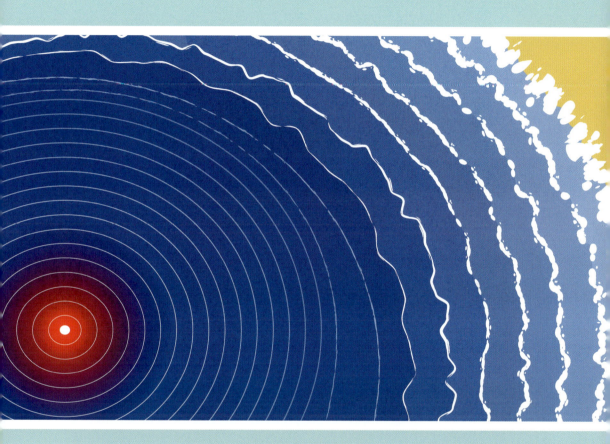

Tsunami waves move outward.

Several events cause tsunamis. The most common cause is an **earthquake**. Earthquakes shake the bottom of the ocean. The ocean floor moves. It makes waves on the surface.

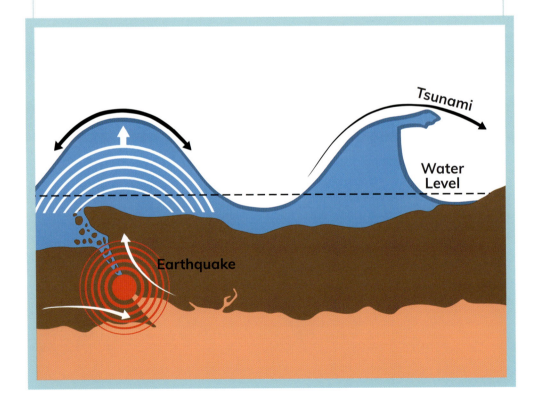

Damage from a tsunami caused by
a volcanic eruption

Volcanoes and **landslides** can also
cause tsunamis.

Tsunamis are not just one big wave. They usually have several waves. This is called a "tsunami wave train." The first wave is not always the largest.

The biggest tsunamis can last for several days. Wave after wave hits the shore.

Tsunami waves move fastest in deep water. In the middle of the ocean, they move at over 500 miles (805 kilometers) per hour. That's faster than an airplane!

Once the waves reach the shore, they slow down. Their speed is 20 to 30 miles (32 to 48 km) per hour. That's the speed of a car driving in town.

Most tsunami waves are less than 10 feet (3 meters) high when they hit land. The biggest tsunami waves can be more than 100 feet (30 m) high. They can cause a lot of damage. They can cause flooding miles from shore.

A scientist measures damage to a tree to find out the height of a tsunami.

But big tsunamis don't happen often. They only happen about twice a year. Smaller tsunamis are like really strong **tides**.

WHERE IN THE WORLD?

Most tsunamis happen in the "Ring of Fire." This area is in the Pacific Ocean. It has lots of activity underground. Many earthquakes and volcanic eruptions happen here. Activity in this area causes three out of every four tsunamis.

RING OF FIRE

Damage from a tsunami in the Mediterranean Sea

Tsunamis have also happened in the Mediterranean Sea, the Caribbean Sea, and the Atlantic Ocean.

Japan, the United States, and Indonesia have the most tsunamis.

The worst tsunami in recent history began in the Indian Ocean in 2004. It started near Indonesia. It hit countries far away in East Africa. It killed more than 200,000 people.

A city in Indonesia was destroyed by a tsunami in 2004.

In 1958, a landslide caused a tsunami in Lituya Bay in Alaska.

Hawaii and Alaska have had many tsunamis. The largest tsunami on record hit Alaska in 1958. It was over 1,720 feet (524 m) high! That is higher than the Empire State Building.

TSUNAMI DANGERS

Tsunamis can be very dangerous. They can cause a lot of damage. The power of the waves is not the only danger. The waves smash buildings and objects. The waves pick up the pieces as they move. This **debris** causes harm as the waves carry it farther onto land.

Debris from an earthquake and a tsunami in Indonesia

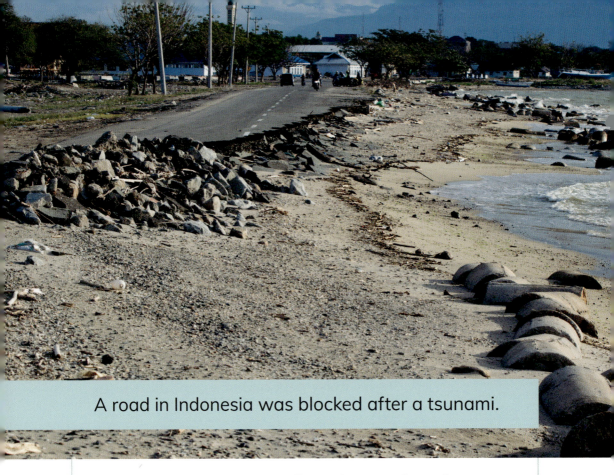

A road in Indonesia was blocked after a tsunami.

Tsunamis cause flooding. Flooding can make drinking water unsafe. Unsafe water can spread disease. There may also be water **shortages**.

Tsunamis can also destroy roads. This makes it hard to deliver rescue supplies.

Tsunamis are bad for the environment. They destroy trees. They destroy animals' homes. And they can spread harmful materials. This pollution can hurt humans and animals. Tsunamis can also **erode** the soil. This can make it hard to grow food.

Birds trapped by debris after a tsunami

BEING PREPARED

Countries in tsunami zones have ways to protect people. Many communities have a warning system. Scientists look for underground activity in the ocean. When they see it, they guess if it will cause a tsunami. They can warn people using sirens and radio messages.

These areas will also have **evacuation** plans. These plans tell people where to go if a tsunami strikes.

People can also build special shelters. The shelters are high above the ground. They keep people safe from the rising water. Shelters are also strong. They can stay standing in earthquakes and powerful waves.

A tsunami evacuation tower in Japan

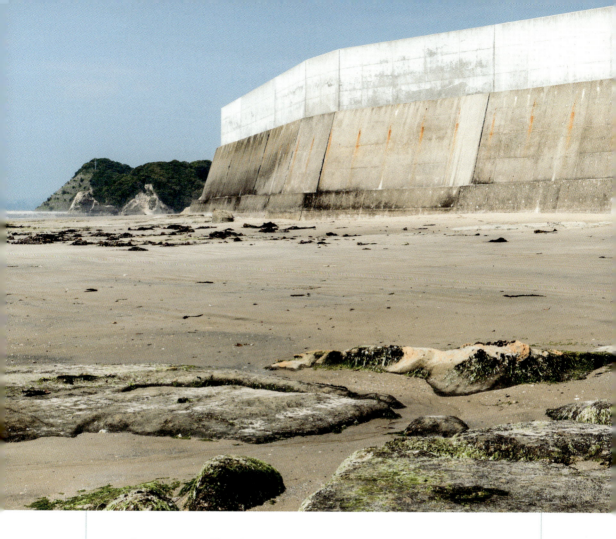

Sea walls help slow the waves. These walls can be 40 feet (12 m) high.

Some communities have created hills and forests near the shore. They work like walls to stop the waves.

TSUNAMI INCOMING!

If you live in a place where tsunamis can happen, know the warning signs. You might feel the ground shaking. The sea level may rise or go down quickly. Or you might hear a loud roar.

Warning signs of a tsunami posted in Barbados in the Caribbean Sea

A warning sign in a tsunami zone in Los Angeles, California

If you notice any of these signs, move away from the shore quickly. Or get to a high building. The farther away from the ocean you are, the safer you will be.

GLOSSARY

debris (duh-BREE)—the pieces of something that has been broken

earthquake (ERTH-kwayk)—the sudden shaking of the Earth's surface

erode (i-ROHD)—to wear away

evacuation (ih-va-kyuh-WAY-shun)—the removal of large numbers of people from an area during a time of danger

harbor (HAR-bur)—a place where ships load and unload their supplies

landslide (LAND-slide)—a large mass of earth and rocks that suddenly slides down a mountain or hill

sea wall (SEE WAL)—a wall that protects land from being damaged by waves

shortage (SHOR-tij)—a situation in which there is not enough of something needed

tide (TIDE)—the rising and falling of the ocean up and down the shore

volcano (vol-KAY-noh)—an opening in the Earth's surface that sometimes sends out hot lava, steam, and ash

READ MORE

Bearce, Stephanie. *Indian Ocean Earthquake and Tsunami*. Lake Elmo, MN: Focus Readers, 2019.

Maurer, Tracy Nelson. *The World's Worst Tsunamis*. North Mankato, MN: Capstone, 2019.

Ventura, Marne. *Detecting Tsunamis*. Lake Elmo, MN: Focus Readers, 2017.

INTERNET SITES

Ducksters: "Earth Science for Kids: Tsunamis" ducksters.com/science/earth_science/tsunamis.php

National Geographic Kids: "Tsunami Facts: Check Out the Mighty Wave!" natgeokids.com/au/discover/geography/physical-geography/tsunamis/

Weather Wiz Kids: "Tsunami" weatherwizkids.com/?page_id=100

INDEX

Alaska, 19

Atlantic Ocean, 17

Barbados, 28

Caribbean Sea, 17, 28

earthquakes, 8, 16, 21, 26

East Africa, 18

evacuation plans, 25

flooding, 14, 22

Hawaii, 19

Indian Ocean, 18

Indonesia, 18, 21, 22

Japan, 4, 5, 18, 26

landslides, 9, 19

Lituya Bay, 19

Los Angeles, California, 29

Mediterranean Sea, 17

ocean, 6, 8, 12, 24, 29

Pacific Ocean, 16

pollution, 23

Ring of Fire, 16

sea walls, 27

shelters, 26

tsunamis
  causes, 8–9
  tsunami wave trains, 10
  warning signs, 28–29
  wave movement, 6–7
  wave size, 10, 14–15
  wave speed, 12

United States, 18

volcanoes, 9, 16

warning systems, 24

ABOUT THE AUTHOR

Isaac Kerry is an author, stay-at-home dad, and firefighter. He lives in Minnesota with his wife, two daughters, and an assortment of cats and dogs. When not engaged in writing, kid wrangling, or extinguishing fires, he loves reading, working out, and playing board games.